Pet Peeves

Also by George Plimpton

The Rabbit's Umbrella

Out of My League

Paper Lion

The Bogey Man

American Journey: The Times of R. F. Kennedy

(with Jean Stein)

Mad Ducks and Bears

One for the Record

One More July

Shadow Box

Sports (with Neil Leiffer)

A Sports Bestiary (with Arnold Roth)

Edie: An American Biography (with Jean Stein)

D.V. (with Christopher Hemphill)

Fireworks: A History and Celebration

Open Net

The Curious Case of Sidd Finch

The X-Factor

Truman Capote

Pet Peeves

or
Whatever Happened
to Doctor Rawff?

George Plimpton

Illustrations by Edward Koren

Altlantic Monthly Press
New York

Published simultaneously in Canada
Printed in the United States of America

FIRST EDITION

Library of Congress Cataloging-in-Publication Data

Plimpton, George.
    Pet Peeves, or, Whatever happened to Doctor Rawff? / George
Plimpton; illustrations Edward Koren
    p. cm.
    ISBN 0-87113-820-4
    I. Veterinarians—Fiction. 2. Pet owners—Fiction 3. Pets—Fiction. I.
Title: Pet peeves. II. Title: Whatever happened to Doctor Rawff? III. Title.

    PS3566.L5 P57 2000
    813'.54—dc21

Designed by Charles Rue Woods and Gretchen Mergenthaler

Atlantic Monthly Press
841 Broadway
New York, NY 10003

00 01 02 03 10 9 8 7 6 5 4 3 2 1

To Laura and Olivia

FOREWORD

As most animal lovers know, Dr. Edmund G. Rawff wrote a biweekly syndicated pet-advice column. He dealt with the myriad questions from readers with authoritative, concise, well-composed answers—putting at ease owners who had written him in despair about their pets' problems. If you wanted to find out how to deal with your dog's mange or a goldfish that insisted on floating upside down, Dr. Rawff was the one to write.

Two years ago, Dr. Rawff wrote his last column and vanished from his modest house in Meriden, Connecticut. He left a note on a hall table that said simply, "I am moving on." In a legal document, he left the house and its furnishings (there were no animals in his care at the time) to the local ASPCA. There was no evidence of foul play. Dr. Rawff had a neighbor who told authorities that he had informed her he was considering giving up his practice, as well as the pet-advice column, pulling up stakes to try something else. Dr. Rawff worked in a small, windowless room in the basement. It was the only room in the house that, upon inspection, seemed in surprising disorder—papers strewn about, a bottle of wine overturned on the desk, an upturned wastepaper basket, broken pencils, crumpled stationery. His framed veterinarian certificate was cracked, as if the doctor had thrown an object at it. One of the ASPCA officials who visited the basement room had the feeling, looking at the disarray, that the doctor had stopped in mid-work and run for the hills as if gas had seeped in from a broken pipe.

The letters strewn about the room included some of those printed here. The crumpled papers turned out to be attempts on Dr. Rawff's part to answer his readers—introductory sentences stating, "I'm not quite sure what to say in reply to yours of . . ." or "I am frankly puzzled by your cat's odd behavior" or "I hardly know what to suggest . . ."

Upon inspection of the readers' letters, more than one ASPCA authority felt that they were written by a single person, composed and sent under different signatures: perhaps with a view to drive the doctor nuts, or at least out of the profession.

Similarities of style were pointed out—the repetition of such phrases as "The question is this." Most of the ASPCA officials scorned this notion, remarking that there was no end to the odd behavior of people's pets, and nothing they read surprised them very much. The order in which the letters appear is arbitrary; none of the letters were dated and the envelopes (surprisingly) were nowhere to be found . . . leading to one further hypothesis—that Dr. Rawff himself might have written the letters for amusement, or perhaps to confuse investigators. Which of these opinions is justified is left entirely to the reader.

—The Editor

DO YOU THINK MY CAT HAS AFFECTION FOR ME?

Dear Dr. Rawff:

My cat has the habit of sleeping on my chest, his face about an inch from mine. I am told this is not uncommon, since cats like to feel the breath on their whiskers, which is why one must be careful about cats getting into cribs and suffocating children. My problem is that my cat weighs forty-five pounds and his breath carries the strong smell of the docks. I am having nightmares in which I am on a fishing trawler, being tossed about in a big storm. Do you think this means my cat has affection for me, or is he trying to suffocate me while I sleep?

—Worried.

Dear Dr. Rawff:

I have a pet but I don't know what it is. Perhaps if I describe it to you, you can help me out. It weighs about a ton. It has a ring in its nose and does a lot of pawing at the living room rug with a hoof. I would think, offhand, that what I have here is a bull, but then again, why on earth would I have a bull as a pet?

—Mystified.

I HAVE A PET, BUT
I DON'T KNOW WHAT IT IS

Dear Dr. Rawff:

I have purchased an attack dog who has been trained to attack at the command "Wisconsin!" Since we live in Wisconsin, the word comes up quite often, especially during the football season. Someone will say, "Next weekend we're going to the Wisconsin-Purdue game," and the dog goes into a frenzy and attacks. Do you know of any way we can deactivate Wisconsin from this dog's neural code, or should we move to Alabama?

—Perplexed.

Dear Dr. Rawff:

I have a dog, whose name is Big Ben, who howls twenty minutes before the hour and does this consistently. Is there any way I can get Big Ben to bark on either the half hour or the hour so that he can be of some service to the community?

—Civic-minded.

Dear Dr. Rawff:

I have a dog who swims only in one direction, which is east. This is all right in small ponds, where he can clamber out at the eastern end, but I'm worried about his future because we hope to settle on the Maryland shore where, if he sets out east, he would not make landfall until Portugal or possibly the Azores. Does this have something to do with the stars? My husband is thinking of moving all three of us to San Diego where if we throw Tubs off a boat he'll swim east and hit the shore. Actually I prefer Maryland. Perhaps the thing to do is let him go east if he insists.

—Ambivalent.

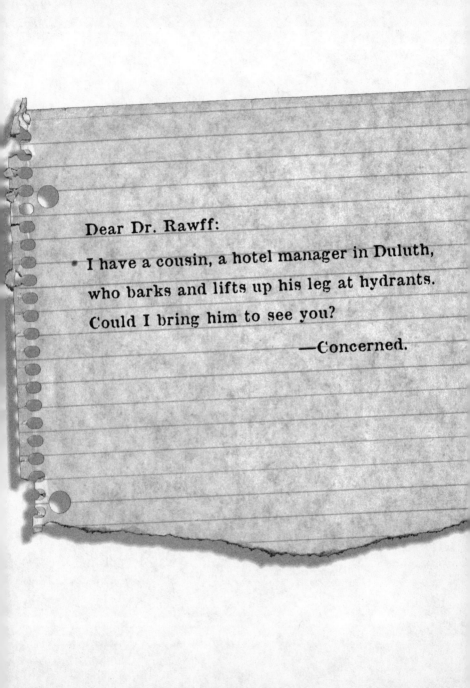

Dear Dr. Rawff:

I have a cousin, a hotel manager in Duluth, who barks and lifts up his leg at hydrants. Could I bring him to see you?

—Concerned.

Dear Dr. Rawff:

I have a goldfish that on occasion jumps out of his bowl and walks around on the carpet on his back fins. I am reminded of something I've seen in nature films. Do I have a rare specimen here?

—Curious.

DO I HAVE A RARE SPECIMEN?

Dear Dr. Rawff:

I wonder if you could help me. I am trying to get my dog into *The Guinness Book of World Records*. My plan is to train Oscar, who is a Scotty, to catch a tennis ball in his mouth dropped from a record height. My dream is to have him catch a tennis ball dropped from a blimp five thousand feet up. My problem is this: I can't get Oscar to catch a ball dropped from a height of *four* feet. He simply lets the ball bounce on the floor. In other words, I have a long ways to go. So does he. Do you think I should change breeds, that I have been training the wrong kind of dog for this sort of thing?

         —Confused.

Dr. Rawff:

I have a pointer who's always pointing at me. I open a door in my house and there he is, tail quivering, stiff as cast iron, his eyes on me. When he's with other people in the family, or with strangers, he romps around like a puppy, but as soon as I put in an appearance, bang! He comes to a point as if I were a huge quail or something. What worries me is that I'm beginning to fancy that he belongs to someone out there with a twelve-gauge shotgun who has designs on bagging me. Can you explain this dog's behavior?

—Worried.

Dear Dr. Rawff:

We have a dog who foams at the mouth. The vet here tells us that he does not have rabies, but simply an excessive saliva production—a behavior phenomenon that he could not explain. In the meantime, Jerry (a spaniel) causes no end of consternation when he runs into a roomful of guests— shouts of dismay, friends heading for the windows, and so on. It does not seem to help when Francis (my husband) and I cry out, "Our dog does *not* have rabies." His condition is so lifelike that friends yell "The hell you say" as they head for the exits. Is there anything you can recommend . . . some kind of pill, perhaps?

—Anguished.

WE HAVE A DOG WHO
FOAMS AT THE MOUTH

Dear Dr. Rawff:

My dog passed away the other day. Jim is (or was) a very old Irish setter. I had no idea what to do with Jim. So I called up the ASPCA and they said they would cremate Jim if I brought him over. So I found a suitcase and managed to get Jim packed in there. I lugged him into the subway. As I was coming up the stairs, this man said, "Ma'am, that bag looks very heavy. Would you like some help with it?" So I said, "Yes, you're very nice." Then this man ran off with my bag with Jim inside. Should I report this to anyone? What do you suppose this man will do when he opens up the suitcase? Do you think I can trust him to take Jim to the ASPCA?

—Anguished.

Dear Dr. Rawff:

I have a dog who never seems to dry off. He can take a swim in August and is still damp in October. He leaves paw marks on the rugs and when he lies in front of the fire he steams. Do you suppose he takes baths without my being aware?

—Bewildered.

Dear Dr. Rawff:

I keep hens. They are always crossing the road to get to the other side. I don't live on the other side. Mr. McGrew lives on the other side. Mr. McGrew keeps hens. His hens are always crossing the road to get to the other side. The question is this: how can I tell whether the hens I'm looking at as I write this are mine or Mr. McGrew's? I'm thinking of painting the legs of my hens with white paint, but suppose what I'm painting are the legs of Mr. McGrew's hens!

—Flummoxed.

Dear Dr. Rawff:

I have bats in the belfry. I am aware that this can mean that I am cuckoo, but the fact is I do have a belfry (I am a schoolteacher living in a converted church) and there are bats in it. My problem is this: I have too many bats in the belfry. But when I go to the proper authorities and complain, "I have bats in the belfry," they reach for the phone and I am taken off to the nearest mental institution. What I want to know is this: should I go through life simply accepting that I have too many bats in the belfry?

—Perturbed.

Dear Dr. Rawff:

I have a dog, a Labrador who doesn't really seem to want to be a dog. He sits down at the piano and plays what sounds to me like one of the motifs from Richard Wagner's *Parsifal*. He takes books out of the library and for all I know is giving himself a liberal arts education. He wears bowler hats and I have seen him settle his paws into my husband's loafers. I think he smokes. The other day I discovered him using the bathroom facilities the way humans do. That was perhaps the last straw—seeing him sitting there. What I want to know is this. Do I have a dog here, or do I have a person who looks like a dog? Please reply.

—Curious.

I THINK HE SMOKES

Dear Dr. Rawff:

I have a hamster. The other day, while I was listening to him run in his Ferris wheel cage—which gives an awful squeak with every revolution—I was struck by an interesting idea. With every turn of his wheel, the hamster is generating power, not much to be sure, but power. Could this be harnessed? Two hamsters would obviously generate twice as much power as one. I have figured out that two hundred and fifty thousand energetic, well-fed hamsters working on shifts in their wheels might very well provide enough power to light the city of Bridgeport, Connecticut. My question is this: do you think the ASPCA would object to the use of hamsters for such a project despite the obvious benefit to the citizens of Bridgeport?

—Civic-minded.

WITH EVERY TURN OF THE WHEEL,
THE HAMSTER IS GENERATING
POWER

Dear Dr. Rawff:

Is Rawff a real name? If you're being clever and trying to imitate a dog's bark, shouldn't it be "Rowff"?

—Inquisitive.

Dear Dr. Rawff:

I have a small dog that I'm beginning to think may be a cat. It was sold to me as a dog. Rather expensive. It meows, catches mice, purrs, and likes milk. Could it be a dog? Or am I living in a fool's paradise . . . ? Please may I hear from you.

—Worried.

Dear Dr. Rawff:

I am thinking of starting a flea circus. The trouble is, I haven't any fleas. I have two dogs, but when I send them into neighborhoods where, in my opinion, they might pick up a flea or two, they come home empty-handed. I look them over. Perhaps they do have fleas, but since I don't see very well (I use a white cane in the streets) I may have missed them. I've heard fleas in flea circuses often carry tiny umbrellas. Do you know where I can find these items? My friends tell me that because of my limited eyesight my flea circus is not a good idea.

—Flustered.

One Lexington Avenue
New York, N.Y. 10010

Dear Dr. Rawff:

I think I have a dog who may be a reincarnation of Marcel Proust. Why do I think this? Well, he takes uncommon interest whenever we have madeleine cookies for tea. He responds when I call out "Marcel" and doesn't when I call "Timmie," which is his given name. He looks French and has a superior attitude when someone like a plumber comes to work in the house. Quite snooty. Do you think I should build him a cork-lined room to see if anything interesting happens in there?

—Wondering.

Dear Dr. Rawff:

Some years ago, I bought a small grayish fish, rather nondescript but interesting-looking, to put in my fish tank. He has been growing, slowly but alarmingly. Last year, after buying increasingly larger tanks, I moved him out of the house into the swimming pool. He cruises around, his fin showing just above the water. Do you think I've done something rather silly?

—Perplexed.

LAST YEAR I MOVED HIM OUT OF THE
HOUSE INTO THE SWIMMING POOL

Dear Dr. Rawff:

My dog has a bark that sounds amazingly like someone shouting "Hands up!" I know that sounds
improbable, but I can assure you that when he barks
in a public park, half the people there (excluding the
children, of course) thrust their arms straight up in
the air. Some people even cry out: "Don't shoot!" Is
there any function you think Beulah might be able
to perform to utilize this aptitude . . . such as a guard
dog in a bank?

—Hopeful.

Dear Dr. Rawff:

My dog seems to like holding his breath. It's a habit he has developed over the years. I have heard of pearl divers in Bali and such places, who can hold their breath for minutes at a time. They have nothing on Spot. I can understand why they do this, but is there not much point in Spot holding his breath. It doesn't seem to serve anyone, much less Spot. I don't think it's very good for his health, do you? His eyes get blood-shot and he exhales with a great burst of noise, often when people are sitting around drinking cocktails. Any suggestions?

—Distressed.

Dear Dr. Rawff:

I am a well-known handler of collies. The other day a Mr. David Letterman, who is the host of a late-night television show, invited my dogs to perform in a feature of his program called "Stupid Pet Tricks." After being assured that "stupid" does not refer to the animals but to the tricks, I allowed one of my prize collies to go to New York City to help out Mr. Letterman. The dog was asked to guide a small flock of sheep off the stage of the Ed Sullivan Theater, down the aisle, out the door onto Forty-fifth Street, and then into a taxi. The collie performed just as I knew he would—keeping the sheep calm and unruffled despite being in the theater and everybody's laughter as he led them out into the street. My problem is this: after Mr. Letterman closed the door of the taxi with the sheep and my dog inside, the taxi driver took off, and I have not seen my dog (or the sheep) since. I have put in a call to the Letterman

turn over ⟶

people. They have informed me that once Mr. Letterman closed the door to the taxi, the dog and the sheep were no longer their responsibility. They were the responsibility of the taxi people. So I called the taxi people. They were not helpful. They felt it very unlikely that any drivers in their fleet would pick up a "herd" of sheep because it was surely against policy. They suspected it was an illegal taxi from New Jersey. It may be that our collie is working the flock through the Lincoln Tunnel on his way here (Duluth, Minnesota) but I think I would have read something about it in the papers. Do you think Mr. Letterman keeps sheep?

—Annoyed.

Dear Dr. Rawff:

I have a pet that was sold to me as a cat. It barks, it likes to balance a ball on its nose, and spends most of its time in a half-filled bathtub upstairs. If I didn't know better I'd think what I have here is something else, but I can't think what.

—Bemused.

Place stamp here

Dear Dr. Rawff:

I have a dog who I have come to believe contains The Word. My reasoning is this: one hot day in August, I happened to notice that when he ran his tongue out to pant, there seemed to be some writing on it, tiny hieroglyphics they seemed to be. I looked closely, and the characters on his tongue looked Chinese. It was my strong conviction that the words, if I could only decipher them, would tell me the secret of life, of the world, of the universe. Alas, I do not speak Chinese. I rushed for a piece of paper and a pencil in order to copy down what I could. What made it difficult was that from time to time he hauled in his tongue to swallow and when he hung it out again, it had a *different* set of Chinese characters. Finally he stopped panting and the writing, The Word if you will, was gone. By some sort of sixth sense, I am utterly convinced my dog has something very big to tell us. I was wondering if any of your other correspondents have had a similar experience, especially those who can read Chinese.

—Expectant.

I HAVE A DOG WHO
I HAVE COME TO BELIEVE
CONTAINS THE WORD

Dear Dr. Rawff:

My husband wrote to you some time ago about a fish in his tank that kept growing until he had to move it into the swimming pool. I'm writing because my husband has disappeared and I keep wondering what your advice to him was. In the meantime I also keep wondering about his fish, which has become so large it can barely make a turn at the end of the pool.

—Worried.

Dear Dr. Rawff:

My cat has no tail. It was sold to me as a Manx, a tailless species, I believe, but mine is rather ferocious and yesterday destroyed a hen. Do you think what I have here might be a lynx?

—Alarmed.

THE TWO MEN HAVE LEFT

Dear Dr. Rawff:

Recently I bought a horse for fifty thousand dollars from a man who said he was an emir. The horse turned out (to my surprise) to be a costume with two men inside, one in the front, the other in the back. The two men have left, leaving me with what they were inside, which is not much. Originally, I was told the horse was a thoroughbred and had won five races and placed twice at Aqueduct Raceway. I'm told that the fifty thousand dollars I paid is a very good price for a horse with that record. So the joke's on me. What I want to know is this: do you know of 1) any two men, perhaps out-of-work actors, willing to be the fore and aft of my horse, and 2) anyone who might like to take a flier in the horse-racing business?

—Hopeful.

Dear Dr. Rawff:

I live on an island (Tortola) in the Caribbean, where I keep two dolphins in a cage attached to the dock. I have trained them to pull a water-sled around the bay with a person aboard. The ride has become a local attraction and is very popular. I have a little postcard stand so people who have taken the ride with the porpoises can send home evidence that they have done so.

The other day I decided to take a ride myself. I hitched up the porpoises and off we went. To my surprise, we left the bay and went bouncing along in the open ocean. I could not get the dolphins to turn. I decided to jump off and swim to shore. But by the time I thought of that, there was no shore in sight to swim for. So I settled down and gave myself over to where the dolphins wanted to go. Night fell—a quite nice moonlit night. Flying fish flew alongside. The next morning we passed a cruise ship, people waving to us from the deck as if it were the most natural thing in the world to see a middle-aged woman being pulled along by two dolphins.

Toward the end of the next day, we spotted a coastline and I was able to land on a sandy beach. A man emerged from under a beach umbrella and asked something that sounded as follows: "Eres en la Seeya?" which I suspect means "Are you in the C.I.A.?"

I believe the language is Spanish. I have two questions. Am I living in Cuba? The second question is this. Is this kind of behavior typical of dolphins? Do you think if I got on the sled, the dolphins will take us home (a homing instinct), or must I consider becoming a citizen of whatever country I'm in?

The dolphins are doing quite nicely, taking people for rides around the local waters. I am being paid in pesos, which must mean something, but people continue to think of me as a foreign agent of some sort. After all, I don't have my passport.

—Muddled.

THEY'VE BEEN AT WORK
FOR THE LAST TEN YEARS

Dear Dr. Rawff:

I have heard a number of times that if you put twenty-five chimpanzees to work at word processors they will eventually, by the laws of chance, type out all the plays of Shakespeare. I have twenty-five chimpanzees at work down in the cellar, working solid eight-hour days. They've been at work for the last ten years. Every night I take a look at what they've done during the day. I have enclosed a typical example:

WYCIITPLLFTHTUZXATTTT
LJLJKHMTYE SGTC TYTYT

What I want to know is this: have I availed myself of chimpanzees with relatively low IQs? Or are they off their feed for some reason? Please advise.

—Curious.

Dear Dr. Rawff:

My cat has an odd limp. It looks as if I spend a lot of time kicking him around. Also, he looks frightened. His face is simply built that way. I'm used to it. Others, though, are aghast. They look at me as if "How could you treat your cat that way?" The reason I'm writing is to ask if there are cosmetic surgeons who might be able to give Tom a less frightened look—a little tightening up of muscles here and there. Do you think this might help or am I doomed to be thought of as a cat-kicker?

—Hopeful.

Dear Dr. Rawff:

I have had an unsettling experience with my bloodhound, Fred. We play this game. After giving him a pair of my old socks as a scent, I hide somewhere around the house and eventually, following my trail, he finds me. It is kind of fun . . . hearing his snuffling getting closer and closer. Wow!

One night not long ago I went out for a long walk in the woods. After a couple of hours, I heard Fred behind me. But then a lot of other dogs' voices joined in. I realized that, led by Fred, they were coming after me. I gave them quite a chase, trying to circle back to my house. On the way, they caught me and put me up a tree. I am writing this from jail. I am here until I can prove I'm not Chuck (One-Thumb) Jackson, a man who held up a bank here a few days ago and fled into the woods. I have two thumbs, but that's of no consequence: I was the one the dogs had treed. Do you think Fred got that posse of fellow-bloodhounds to come after me because he thought it was funny? Or do you have a more pessimistic view?

—At a loss.

Dear Dr. Rawff:

I have a long-maned white horse with a horn sticking out of its forehead. My friends tell me that what I have here is a narwhal, but I always thought that narwhals lived in the Arctic Ocean. What is going on here?

—Bewildered.

WHAT'S GOING ON HERE?

Dear Dr. Rawff:

I have a horse who's always getting up on things, like carts. My theory is that, having been ridden all his life, he now wants to ride something—just to find out what it's like. I got a hint of this when I found him in the garage, standing on the wreck of a tricycle that obviously couldn't contain his weight. Next, I found him standing in my Buick convertible. I love Ned, but from time to time I have these nightmares that one day he'll throw a saddle on me and climb aboard. Am I just a worrywart?

—Confused.

Dear Dr. Rawff:

You may remember me as the one who wrote to you about my twenty-five chimpanzees typing in the cellar and how disappointed I was that nothing like Shakespeare's plays was being produced at all—gibberish for ten years and a big waste of paper. But the other day I went down there and discovered that the chimpanzees were working on a legible manuscript, which I am convinced is the ending of *Edwin Drood*, the novel Charles Dickens never finished. What I want to know is this: do you think the completed *Edwin Drood* has a better chance of being published if it is sent in under the name of Charles Dickens alone, or Charles Dickens & Twenty-five Chimpanzees?

—Puzzled.

Dear Dr. Rawff:

You'll never guess what kind of pets I have. Falcons! Last week I bought a pair from an emir at the airport. He had them on his arm. They came with these little hoods on. He told me that once you take off the hoods the birds fly off your arm and stoop (I think that was the word) on rabbits and hares and gazelles, although we don't have the latter two species in Wilton, Connecticut. But we do have rabbits galore, so I thought falcons would be just the thing! But when I took the falcons out onto the lawn in front of the house and took their hoods off, they stared at me reproachfully. They didn't budge. When I pointed out the rabbits eating the roses at the edge of the lawn, they gave not the slightest notice. Is there a command you give the falcon when you take the hood off, such as "Fetch!"? I tried that but it didn't work.

My neighbor came by the other day and said, "That's a nice pair of Rhode Island Reds you've got there. Why are they wearing those little caps?"

Do you think the emir got away with something? I'm beginning to wonder.

—Anxious.

LAST WEEK I BOUGHT A
PAIR FROM AN EMIR
AT THE AIRPORT

Dear Dr. Rawff:

My chimpanzees, having finished *Edwin Drood,* have come up with a manuscript that could very well be F. Scott Fitzgerald's missing final chapters of *The Last Tycoon.* I'm not sure about this because they haven't finished it yet, but it seems to me to fit. What's next? Do you suppose it might be the famous second part of Gogol's *Dead Souls,* which he is supposed to have burned just before he climbed into bed and died?

—Excited.

Dear Dr. Rawff:

I am an emir passing through town. I have oil money. I have an odd request. Do you keep hens, Rhode Island Reds, or if not, do you know where I can get my hands on some?

—Praise be to Allah.

Dear Dr. Rawff:

I suspect a lot of money can be made out of a circus act involving a dog (in this case my Saint Bernard) emerging from a cannon mouth and landing in a net on the far side of the circus arena. Crowds would go wild. Do you think it's too much to ask of my dog (Wally) to go into partnership with an act of this sort? I await your reply.

—Hopeful.

I SUSPECT THAT A LOT
OF MONEY CAN BE MADE
OUT OF A CIRCUS ACT
INVOLVING A DOG

Dear Dr. Rawff:

I have always heard that goats eat tin cans. I have set out tin cans for my goat, but she turns up her nose at them. Naturally, I have tried different kinds of cans, thinking that was the problem. A friend of mine says what I have is not a goat but an impala, an African antelope. Since the one I have doesn't eat tin cans, I would have to suppose that by rational reasoning my friend is correct. But before telling my friends that what I have out in the backyard is an impala, I would like to know if there is such a thing as a non-can-eating goat. Otherwise I have an impala, which is not what I ordered from Higbee Farms.

—Disconcerted.

Dear Dr. Rawff:

I have a mournful elkhound. I thought his melancholy frame of mind—sleeping all day long and moaning from time to time in the most awful way—was because he is unable to practice what he is bred to do: chase elks. Because of the elkhound, I moved away to a farm near Elmira and I bought an elk. It lives out back in an enclosure. The elkhound has taken no notice of the elk. He continues to moon around the house. The elk doesn't look any happier. To compound matters, my cousin Alex, who is going away to Europe, just sent me Tombo, a wolfhound who is even more morose than the elkhound, much less the elk. I fully appreciate that if I get a wolf for the enclosure back there, it may well improve Tombo's sense of well-being, but hardly the elk's. What I'm really asking is, How do you make unhappy animals happy?

—Despondent.

TO OUR SURPRISE, JONES SURVIVED

Dear Dr. Rawff—

I have a Labrador retriever. An avid duck
hunter, I have used him with great success
over the years. Last year, a friend and I took
our van out onto a frozen lake. After we got
our guns out, my friend took a stick of dynamite from the van, lit its long fuse, and sent it
scaling out over the ice—the idea, of course,
to bust open a hole in the ice for the ducks to
come in to. As we watched the dynamite skit-
tering toward the middle of the lake, suddenly
we noticed that our retriever was after it! We
yelled at him—"Come back! Come back!"
These are not commands that he has ever
heard. We watched him reach the dynamite
and, with the stick sideways in his mouth, he
started trotting back toward us. So we shouted
at him to go back, making shooing motions
with our hands. He just kept coming. We
picked up our shotguns and started firing at

turn over ⟶

him. It was a question of him or us. We could see the chips of ice flying up around him as he came. Poor dog! He veered away and went and *hid under the van!*

After a second or so there was a huge explosion. The van sort of rose up in the air, and then sank in the lake. To our surprise, Jones survived. He had dropped the stick of dynamite and escaped on the far side.

These days he sulks around the house looking distrustful. He refuses to retrieve. When I pick up anything that looks like a stick, he hides under the house. I am writing to ask if you can think of a program of therapy that might get us back the retriever we know and love, not this sniveler.

—Anxious.

Dear Dr. Rawff:

I have an eight-hundred-pound gorilla. I take him on trips. We stop at motels. I say to the man behind the desk, "Where's my eight-hundred-pound gorilla going to sleep?" The guy behind the desk looks at my eight-hundred-pound gorilla and then he pulls out a key and says: "Room 160."

My gorilla is upset by this. Isn't the guy behind the desk supposed to say "Anywhere he wants"? The result of this is that my eight-hundred-pound gorilla is not only losing his self-esteem but his weight. If this keeps up I'll be able to sell him to an organ-grinder. Please advise.

—Troubled.

Dear Dr. Rawff:

My boyfriend has a sheepdog who sheds, especially when the winter is over and he starts molting. The other day, just to be helpful, I was pulling a grooming brush through his fur and I combed out a hair clip, a bedroom slipper, a false eyelash, a lipstick tube, a bible, and a champagne glass. I have been worried because I think my boyfriend has his eye on the preacher's daughter who sings in the choir. Do you think this means he's spending time with her, or am I imagining things?

—Suspicious.

Dear Dr. Rawff:

You might be interested to know that I have taken my chimpanzees off their word processors, now that they have finished (at least to my satisfaction) *Edwin Drood*, *The Last Tycoon*, and *Dead Souls*, and have sat them down at twenty-five pianos. The din down in the cellar is frightening at the moment, but I see no reason, given their past success with literature, why they should not give us in time the ending to Schubert's *Unfinished Symphony*.

—Elated.

Dear Dr. Rawff:

In the basement I have an alligator who is getting longer. At feeding time I open the cellar door (we live in a town house on Sixty-third Street) and throw things down. Then I close the door. But the other day I opened up the cellar door and I saw two big alligators down there. What I want to know is this: I've always heard that little pet alligators were often flushed down the toilet when their owners went away to live in Memphis or whatever and that down in the sewers of New York they grew to enormous sizes. Is it possible that my alligator is a female and that these sewer alligators are using my basement as a breeding ground? I am putting the best face on all of this. What I have down there may be New York's first alligator farm! Would you think of going into business with me?

—Hopeful.

AT FEEDING TIME I OPEN
THE CELLAR DOOR...
AND THROW THINGS DOWN

Dear Dr. Rawff:

Do you know anyone
who would like an ibex?
I've discovered they're
just not much fun.

—Downcast.

I'VE DISCOVERED THEY'RE NOT MUCH FUN

Dear Dr. Rawff:

I have, on occasion, the unquenchable desire to kiss this frog we have in our fishpond out back. Whether I can—at the moment of truth—go through with it, I don't know, and nor do I know how the frog feels about it. It may take a *lunge* on my part and quite a disruption in the pond itself if I can't connect. What I want to know is this: if Prince Charles or someone of that ilk suddenly appears because of the kiss, is there some way of sending the prince (or others) back as unwanted if I don't like them? I have enough problems in my house without Prince Charles tracking in water-lily stems from the fishpond. And yet, there's the frog, waiting. . . . Please advise.

—Romantic.

Dear Dr. Rawff:

I have an interesting idea. And that is to introduce feral poodles into Yellowstone National Park. My reason is this: variety is the spice of life, and while the animal population in Yellowstone is interesting (grizzlies, chipmunks, and so on), more is better, wouldn't you agree? My problem is this: how do you make a poodle feral? I know there is a procedure for introducing wild animals to the wilds (quite simple, I would think), but how about poodles?

—Interested citizen.

I HAVE A PARROT I'M TRYING TO TEACH

Dear Dr. Rawff:

I have a parrot I'm trying to teach to say as follows:

> In Xanadu did Kubla Khan
> A stately pleasure-dome decree:
> Where Alph . . .

The trouble is this: when the guests are assembled to hear my remarkable parrot and the moment is upon us, the parrot says as follows:

> I will arise and go now, and go to Innisfree,
> And a small cabin build there, of clay and
> wattles made:
> Nine bean rows . . .

There are those who might say that a parrot is remarkable enough who can quote, and at great length, William Butler Yeats. The problem is this: I don't like Yeats, and, as far as I'm concerned, the parrot can stay down there in Yeats's "foul rag and bone shop of the heart" unless he pulls himself together and gets with it with Coleridge.

—Chagrined.

Dear Dr. Rawff:

Hi! I'm the one who brought you Meg, my boa constrictor, who had swallowed Bobby, my pig, and you were able to extricate Bobby before he got too far down, and though he tends to shake a bit in his dreams, I think he's OK. Meg is fine too. I think you looked tired, Dr. Rawff, and in need of a vacation or at least some chicken soup. I liked the way you talked to Bobby as he slowly reemerged. You're a good man, Dr. Rawff, much nicer than my ex-husband, who would have let Meg have her way.

—Lovingly.

Dear Dr. Rawff:

I am the one who wrote to you about the dog that lived in the hen house and wouldn't come out. You recommended I sell the dog. I did so, which left me without a dog. I wrote to ask you what to do then, and you suggested I get another dog. So I did. And when we got home, the dog went right into the hen house. It turns out I bought the same dog I had before. So much for your suggestions! Thanks but no thanks!

—Angry.

MY DOG SEEMS TO BE
COLOR~BLIND

Dear Dr. Rawff:

My dog seems to be color-blind. He hauls me across streets when the lights are against us. Are there glasses that can correct this problem? I don't think there's any design in what he does . . . I mean I don't think he's trying to get rid of me or anything. Of course, there was that time in the kitchen when he turned on the gas with his paw. But I think he was trying to tell me he was hungry.

—Worried.

Dear Dr. Rawff:

The other day I brought home two rabbits for my daughter. They were sitting on a bed of lettuce in a cardboard box in the backseat of my car. By error, I locked myself out of the garage and couldn't get back in until the following morning. I looked in the box and discovered, somewhat to my surprise, only one rabbit. I have searched everywhere for the other rabbit—the car, the garage. I know this may seem a stupid question, but is it possible that the rabbit *ate* the other one?

—Confounded.

I LOOKED IN THE BOX AND
DISCOVERED SOMEWHAT TO
MY SURPRISE ONLY ONE
RABBIT

Dear Dr. Rawff:

I have a problem. I am the president of our co-op on Seventy-second Street. We have planted a row of privet bushes in front of the building, neatly trimmed. Every day a gentleman walking three spaniels on their leashes comes to our block and waters them against these bushes. Spotting this from an upstairs window, I have rushed out and protested that the bushes will die if his dogs continue to do this. He is a Frenchman. He says the bushes are God's bushes. I say the bushes are our bushes, because we paid for them. He says this is not logical. He is a Cartesian Frenchman and very likely a communist. Moreover, he is a large Frenchman, in a big coat, and there is no way that I can physically have my way. I have said so to my husband, an ex-Syracuse fullback, who is usually sitting in front of the television set watching a soap opera.

I say to him that what I want him to do is rush out onto Seventy-second Street when the Frenchman

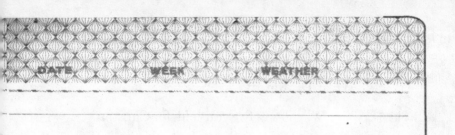

brings his dogs by, and pee on them, not the Frenchman, but his dogs. My husband is against this. He looks up from the soap opera and he asks me as follows: "Do you really think I am going to get up from this soap opera and run down Seventy-second Street trying to pee on three spaniels belonging to a Frenchman?" What I want to know is this, considering his attitude: is my husband no longer in love with me or is he a no-good wastrel couch potato?

—Concerned botanist.

Dear Dr. Rawff:

When I was five years old, for Christmas I was given a goldfish in a bowl with the instructions that I was to care for it, and that if I didn't, it would die. Although it was not clear at the time exactly what that meant, I did what I was told. I dropped in feed for the goldfish, cleaned the bowl, put some vegetation in there, and a little castle, and after six months the goldfish floated up to the top of the water and died. So then my parents gave me a zebra finch in a cage, and they told me that if I didn't take care of it, it would die. So I put the seed in a little dish, put up something for it to scratch its beak on, and a mirror to look at itself in, and I changed the paper in the bottom of the cage every week. After six months it died. Then came a hamster. The instructions were the same. So I cared for the hamster and fed it and oiled the wheel it ran around in, and after the hamster passed on, I got a cat that, after two years of care and feeding, while sleeping on a sofa, was sat upon by a police officer. In there somewhere I have owned a frog, a turtle, two dogs, all of whom despite my ministrations and worry were taken from me (one of the dogs died under a Zamboni ice-rink cleaner) in circumstances too complicated for me to go into. I have had pet hens, lizards. The other day my father told me that he was thinking of getting me a horse. I'm not sure about the horse. I took out a pad and a pencil and figured out that since the age of five—I am eighteen—I have spent a total (walking the dogs being the largest commitment) of 4,475 hours looking after animals—almost a year, if you subtract hours spent asleep. What I want to know is this: do you think my time would have been better spent if I'd learned something substantial, such as taking lessons on how to play the harp?

—Puzzled teenager.

MY DOG LIKES TO BE CARRIED
AROUND IN A BAG

Dear Dr. Rawff:

My dog likes to be carried around in a bag. I think he got the idea because he caught sight of a woman carrying a Chihuahua around in a purse. The trouble is that my dog is a large Airedale who weighs about thirty pounds. I have found a large canvas bag used for carrying firewood in which I can fit Junior (his name). He loves it. But I wonder, Dr. Rawff, if you've ever carried a large Airedale around in a bag. It is backbreaking work. Will it cause psychic damage if I don't give in to Junior's wishes?

—Exhausted.

Dear Dr. Rawff:

Hi! It's me again. I'm the one who came in with Meg who had started to swallow Bobby, the pig, for the second time. Once again, you were able to separate the two with such wonderful skill. I liked the way you lectured Meg—"No more of that!" I just died! I think you're probably right. It's not a good idea keeping Meg and Bobby in the same cage. I thought the two were friends, but I guess not.

Thank you for tea. I was worried, all those crumpled pieces of paper lying around the floor. They made me think you're overstressed, and I can see why: people like me coming in with Meg and Bobby.

We are moving to Racine, Wisconsin. I hope you will drop in if the occasion arises, especially if Meg and Bobby get into trouble again. Really sincerely.

—Thankfully.

AFTERWORD

A careful reading of the letters might suggest that Dr. Rawff left to join the woman who was having the trouble with the boa constrictor, Meg, and Bobby, the pig. She's the only one of the letter writers who has turned up in his office. They had tea. She seems quite sweet on him and urges him to come to Racine, Wisconsin. Perhaps, though, like the young woman who wrote about spending too many hours in the care of animals, he has left the veterinarian practice to take up something else. Could it be that he has gone to rescue the woman who was towed to a strange exotic island by her pet dolphins? Perhaps he's dropped in on the man whose chimpanzees have completed three unfinished works and are now at work on Schubert's *Unfinished*. Or to check on the woman who wrote in about the "narwhal." Or perhaps on the woman with the huge fish in her swimming pool. On the other hand, maybe he wrote the letters to himself in order to throw off anyone curious enough to wonder about his disappearance. It may well be that he will simply turn up back in his office after an extended vacation and hang out his shingle once more. Perhaps not, though. After all, the postman comes up the street once a day, except Sundays . . .